The Body's Business

by Rebecca Weber

Content Adviser: September Kirby, CNS, MS, RN,
Instructor, Health Promotion and Wellness,
South Dakota State University

Reading Adviser: Rosemary G. Palmer, Ph.D.,
Department of Literacy, College of Education,
Boise State University

Spyglass
BOOKS

COMPASS POINT BOOKS

Minneapolis, Minnesota

Compass Point Books
3109 West 50th Street, #115
Minneapolis, MN 55410

Visit Compass Point Books on the Internet at *www.compasspointbooks.com*
or e-mail your request to *custserv@compasspointbooks.com*

Photographs ©: Rubberball, cover; Image Source, 4, 5; Corbis, 7, 20 (top);
Brand X Pictures, 9, 13, 17; Comstock, 11; Mug Shots/Corbis, 14; Thinkstock, 15;
LWA-Dann Tardif/Corbis, 19; Digital Vision, 20 (bottom); Stockbyte, 21 (top, bottom).

Editor: Patricia Stockland
Photo Researcher: Marcie C. Spence
Designer: Jaime Martens

Library of Congress Cataloging-in-Publication Data
Weber, Rebecca.
  The body's business / by Rebecca Weber.
      p. cm. — (Spyglass books)
  Summary: Introduces how the human body processes food into energy and
  how the various parts of the body work together to function as a whole.
  Includes bibliographical references and index.
  ISBN 0-7565-0622-0 (hardcover)
  1. Body, Human—Juvenile literature. 2. Human physiology—Juvenile literature.
  [1. Body, Human. 2. Human physiology.] I. Title. II. Series.
  QP37.W38 2004
  612—dc22   2003014477

Contents

NOTE: Glossary words are in **bold** the first time they appear.

Your Body

Your body's main job is to keep you alive.

Even when you are sleeping, your body is still working. It is just like a factory.

A Day at a Factory

A bakery takes in flour and turns it into bread. Your body takes in food and air. It turns them into *energy*.

A Busy Brain

Your brain does an important job. Your brain tells your body what to do. If you are reading, your brain tells you what your eyes are seeing. It tells your heart to keep beating.

Small but Powerful

By the time you are 6 years old, your brain weighs about 3 pounds (1.4 kilograms). That is as heavy as it will ever get.

Heart Healthy

Your heart does an important job. Your heart pumps blood through your body. Blood carries in *nutrients* and *oxygen.* It carries out *waste.* Your heart pumps all the time.

Two Pumps

The right side of your heart pumps blood to your lungs to get oxygen. Then the left side pumps that blood to the rest of your body.

9

Love Your Lungs

Your lungs do an important job. When you breathe in, your lungs pull in air to get oxygen. Then the oxygen is sent through your body. When you breathe out, your lungs get rid of the used air.

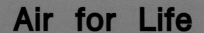

Air for Life

You cannot live without air. If your brain does not have oxygen for three minutes, it starts to die.

The Food Track

Your digestive system does an important job. These *organs* take in food and get rid of waste. Your body gets nutrients from food.

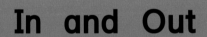

In and Out

Food moves from your stomach to your small intestine to your blood. Leftovers are sent out through your large intestine.

Sensible Senses

Your senses do an important job. Hearing, seeing, smelling, touching, and tasting are all senses. They tell you what is going on around you.

Stand Up Straight

Your ears do more than hear things. Tiny bones in your ears help you keep your *balance.*

Big, Strong Bones

Your bones do an important job. Your bones help you move. They keep your organs safe. Many of your muscles are attached to your bones. These muscles move your bones by pulling on them.

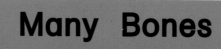

Many Bones

By the time you grow up, you will have about 206 bones. Half of these are in your hands and feet!

The Skin You Are In

Your skin does an important job. It keeps your blood and organs inside your body. It also keeps out germs and dirt. When you play hard, your skin makes sweat that cools you down.

Save That Skin
Always make sure you wear sunscreen. This will help your skin stay safe from the sun.

19

Fun Facts

The left side of your brain controls the right side of your body. The right side of your brain controls the left side of your body.

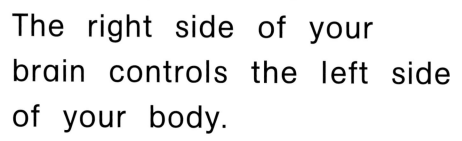

Messages to and from your brain can travel more than 200 miles (320 kilometers) per hour.

Your teeth have different jobs. Front teeth tear food apart. Back teeth mash and grind food so you can swallow it.

Always try to breathe through your nose. It has thousands of little hairs that trap dust and dirt.

Glossary

balance–a sense that helps people stay upright

energy–a force that gives something the power to grow or move

nutrients–the small parts of food, water, and air that a living thing needs to stay alive and grow

organs–the soft parts of your body that do work that keeps you alive

oxygen–a part of the air that people breathe in, and what people need to stay alive

waste–something that has been used up or that cannot be used

Learn More

Books

Conrad, David. *Burps, Boogers, and Bad Breath.* Minneapolis: Compass Point Books, 2002.

Seuling, Barbara. *From Head to Toe: The Amazing Human Body and How It Works.* New York: Holiday House, 2002.

On the Web

For more information on The Body's Business, use FactHound to track down Web sites related to this book.

1. Go to *www.compasspointbooks.com/facthound*
2. Type in this book ID: 0756506220
3. Click on the *Fetch It* button. Your trusty FactHound will fetch the best Web sites for you!

Index

GR: K
Word Count: 241

From Rebecca Weber

The world is such a great place!
I love teaching kids how to take
care of themselves and take
care of nature.